Hearts
HAVE REASONS

Hearts HAVE REASONS

Jim Meehan

ThomasMore®
– An RCL Company –

Send all inquiries to:
Thomas More Publishing
An RCL Company
200 East Bethany Drive
Allen, Texas 75002-3804

BOOKSTORES:
   Call Bookworld Companies 888-444-2524 or fax 941-753-9396
PARISHES AND SCHOOLS:
   Thomas More Publishing 800-822-6701 or fax 800-688-8356
INTERNATIONAL:
   Fax Thomas More Publishing 972-264-3719

Printed in the United States of America

Library of Congress Catalog Card Number 99-85804

ISBN 0-88347-451-4

1 2 3 4 5   04 03 02 01 00

This work is dedicated
to the three women
in my life

my wife Maureen
my daughter Larissa
my mother Pearl

Contents

Preface

There is a tendency, at times, for us to place a sharp divide between our feelings and emotions on the one hand and our thinking and willing on the other—the heart metaphorically representing the seat of the former and the reason representing the seat of the latter. We often talk of the body and the mind or the heart and the head in this connection.

On many occasions, even before becoming a psychologist, this distinction became blurred for me as feelings, emotions, and ideas interplayed and converged. When trying to express such interactive states, the form that found favor was verse. Rhythm, rhyme, and the sound and meaning of words enabled feelings, emotions, and ideas to be captured, encapsulated, and conveyed.

Many people, on coming across the verses, have urged me to publish and thus share my feelings, emotions, and thoughts with a wider audience.

Hearts Have Reasons is the title given to the resultant collection of verses. The title is used to stress the interdependence between physical feelings and moods and the intellectual functions of cognition and conation. When our first reactions come from the heart, we must be patient and attend carefully, for hearts have reasons which often only become apparent later, usually as a result of analysis or reflection. Intuitions are not mindless but need to be evaluated to ensure that they are correct and appropriate. It was Blaise Pascal (1623-1662) who wrote: *Le coeur a ses raisons que la raison ne connait pas*. The heart has its reasons of which reason knows nothing(Pensées IV 277).

Acknowledgments

With her usual amazing speed and accuracy, endless patience and a sense of humor, Michelle Fulmer typed repeated drafts and constantly improved the format of the manuscript.

A number of close colleagues read, critiqued, and worked on these various drafts and provided invaluable advice and assistance.

Friends and relatives have encouraged me by their kind words, particularly my wife Maureen and Lynn and Barry Green.

Several other people generously contributed, in various ways, to the eventual publication and wish to remain anonymous.

Many people have, in expressing their ideas and in living their lives, provided the stimuli that awaken the need to capture these values in verse.

Thank you all for your help freely given.

Introduction

The verses in this book are arranged in chronological order, and, in effect, reflect stages in an ongoing journey that began in 1965. To help readers, in some measure, understand the wider context of this journey, some biographical background is provided.

At the age of twenty-two, following four and a half years of studying philosophy and theology at the seminary, I realized that I did not have a priestly calling. Accordingly, I began a search for an appropriate career and, after some experimentation, two years later in 1967, I selected a position in personnel management. As part of my professional studies, I was introduced to social and industrial psychology and became absorbed in the study of people and relationships in the workplace.

In 1969, I met Maureen, my wife-to-be, and started to concentrate more on relationships outside of pure occupational settings. We married in 1971 and Larissa, our only child, was born in 1974.

Prompted by a desire to learn more about people, in 1982 I began a course with the Open University, majoring in psychology, which was followed by a Master's in the

Applications of Psychology from the Health Sciences department of what is now Wolverhampton University.

In 1991, I left the field of personnel management to work full-time as an occupational psychologist. I spent two years in the United States, during which time I worked for a remarkably altruistic person, Dr. William E. Hall, in Atlanta, Georgia. He specialized in the theory and practice of human relationships, the study of success, and he emphasized the benefits to be accrued by encouraging people to concentrate more on their strengths and to do more of what they are good at doing and enjoy. It was a privilege to work with such a positive and insightful man who was so very generous in sharing his life's work.

In addition to the above backdrop, the immediate context of each individual piece is provided on the page facing it.

The use of the term *man* is often meant to refer to mankind, and the use of the masculine personal pronoun is not meant to rule out females or, when used to refer to God, to suggest that God has a sex.

(1) This saying has been attributed to many authors, most especially to Stephen Grellet (1773-1853), although it has not been found in any of his writings.

"*I* expect to pass through this world but once, any good thing, therefore, I can do, or any kindness that I can show to any fellow creature, let me do it now, let me not defer or neglect it, for I shall not pass this way again."

Proverbial Saying (1)

"*A* little kindness from one person to another is better than a vast love for all mankind."

Anonymous

After nearly four years of preparing for a celibate priesthood,
I decided to pursue the vocation of marriage.

The liturgical year aptly reflected time I spent in the wilderness
of my soul, struggling with critical directional issues. These gave
way, at last, to the hope of a shared life and a new mission.

March 1965

On Leaving Seminary

Loneliness and listlessness are the symptoms
    of my discontent.

It's as though every day were Ash Wednesday
    and life a continuous Lent!

Please God, I'll meet a woman who can love me
    and be loved.

To me she'll be my Easter and fiery Pentecost.

Relationships require the risk of being rejected and the risk of being accepted.

The mysterious dynamics of interdependency must be recognized.

The manner in which one person relates to another certainly holds the key to the future—whether it is to inspire or to denigrate, to lead or to drive, to love or to hate.

January 1966

Altruism

In order that man himself may know,
To others his personality he must show.
'Tis a journey often fraught with frustration,
     disillusion and toil,
Rejected love into his inner self makes man recoil.

Introspection is a preoccupation
     that tends to despair.
And once again, he is forced to scuttle
     from his egotistic lair.
This time he will more warily tread,
     not so easily led
To emulate the ostrich and, in his own misery,
     bury his head.

Goodness is diffusive of itself;
And by others, man's goodness will indeed be felt.
And as the seed must die before the plant can grow,
So in part, from himself, man must outward flow.

At this point, the search for a meaningful career plan posed more fundamental questions for me to answer.

July 1966

Motivation

Have you ever felt the need
To give yourself in thought, word, and deed
To someone, to something, an ideal?

Is this feeling the seed of love
Planted in man's nature from above,
To flower in peace and not in blood?

Is it in essence pure,
Existing to placate man's restlessness and provide the cure
To the present mass disease of hiding behind a selfish door?

If it is, then give way to its swell,
Be transformed by its life-giving spell,
Or else the world will become an egocentric and
    individualistic hell!

Having been rejected by a girlfriend after an eighteen-month courtship, I searched for the root causes.

Did we really know each other?
Was it intentional?
Was it inevitable?

January 1968

Sincerity

Why is it so difficult for man to be sincere,
lack sham, deceit, and pretense?
Is it because his true self he does not revere?
Or to self-deception is there no defense?

At last—bells and banjos!
This was no mere infatuation!

June 1970

My Future Wife

Masked majesty is mirrored in a certain human screen,
Which in others reflects merely what can be seen.
But there is something special about this certain queen,
Who meanders through life—my dearest Maureen.

The seventies were coming to a close. The end of a busy decade in terms of family events, professional growth, and adjustment. It was a period during which I underwent five surgical operations, two of which involved my right internal ear.

Certainly, I felt a yearning for more simplicity.

Christmas 1979

Insight

Often, when the commonplace is touched by the hand of a
    genius, great beauty appears.

Often, simplicity lies at the root of man's greatest ideas.

Often, reality is masked by layers of sophisticated
    intellectual veneers,

Awaiting an incisive mind to penetrate and clear.

I spent much time living in my head. After a hectic fifteen months at work involving plant closures leading to five or six thousand people losing their jobs, I again needed to take stock of my beliefs and behavior.

June 1981

Living Faith

Confused by the conflicting claims of differing religious and
    philosophical theories,
I search blindly for the meaning of life.
Perhaps the endeavor would reach an early conclusion if I
    abandoned "isms" and "ologies"
And just helped people in their daily strife.
Perhaps helping others (liked or not), whatever their need,
Would lead to something more than a
    pure humanistic creed.
Perhaps deeds, not data, will give me cause to believe.
Loving should LOVE more easily reveal.
But as persons are known by what they say and do,
Perhaps we have to read the various scriptures too!
Yes! Faith must arise from both reading and
    acts of charity—
Mixed according to each man's priority.

Larissa is ten years old now and it was very enjoyable helping her with her homework.

One assignment she had to write a poem about Autumn, which prompted me to present a parallel parental view.

November 1984

Autumn's Renewal

Is it because winter nears
That most trees shed their leafy tears?
Is it because summer's gone
That it's no longer warm?
Is it because the trees are tired
That they can't hold their blooms so long?
Or is it that they require
More fresh sap to keep them strong?
Is there any reason at all
Why things are the way they are?
Some answers, however small,
Beyond "que sera sera"?
Many birds see in this fall
Nature's sign to take the air
Answering their autumnal call
To seek warmth and sun elsewhere!
Leaving us behind to stare
At the browns, yellows, and golds
That remind us every year
That we, like trees, grow old.

A time to take stock of time
And retreat from life's pressures;
To renew rhythm and rhyme
And realize life's treasures.
Autumn signals winter's cold
And nature slows down its pace.
Shorter days and longer nights unfold,
Less daytime in which to race.

Larissa wrote an essay about me. Later that evening, I stole some of her words and shaped them into verse.

January 1985

A Portrait of a Father

(With the help of words from my primary school daughter)

My daddy's very special and also very kind.
He has a very special way to make me change my mind.
When I want to do something he doesn't want me to do,
He gives me all his reasons then adds, "It's really up to you."

I'm sure his job is important—working as he
    does in personnel!
He sees a lot of people—and goes to meetings as well.
Though he works in a company where many cars are made,
He always says "Dealing with people problems
    is my true trade."

When he's not at work he's always reading psychology,
And he's worked very hard to get his honors degree.
Well, he'll need to use this knowledge,
    every last little bit—
In order to discover what makes his darling daughter tick.

I turn another of Larissa's projects into verse that echoes a search for meaning.

April 1985

Time and Time Again

As our planet whirls through space at breakneck speed,
Ploughing through a sea of time,
Many passengers no longer feel the need
To know what's at the end of the line.

Why are we on this spaceship earth and where are
    we journeying to?
Does death bring an end to what we know as time?
Who built this blue craft, and is there a purpose for the crew?
Is there any reason or any rhyme?

Forward, forward, relentlessly and remorselessly we go,
Leaving memories, dates, and distance behind.
How remarkable it is to know.
The only way backward is through the mind.

The mind is the only time machine we possess,
If machine it can indeed be called.
So let us use it carefully to assess
The past, the present—and predict what the future will hold.

Do we seek God outside ourselves as many Western religions advocate?

Or is God to be found by looking within ourselves as many Eastern religions teach?

Perhaps both are correct. In this poem I attempt to reconcile the two traditions.

While holding on to the real distinction between finite and infinite being and avoiding a pantheistic view, the two types of being are nevertheless mysteriously related—not least in that they are both beings.

Thomas Aquinas wrote about the analogy of being. The two types of being are the same, yet different, as is the meaning of *foot* in the phrase "the foot of the mountain."

Finite and infinite being are in some way the same, yet different. God, Infinite Being, is too great to be understood or fitted into the human brain or mind or head.

We can empathize with others because we are members of the same species, although each individual is unique.

This is also the case in our relationship with God.

December 1986

Being in Being

Infinite being plus one is an impossibility we are told
By mathematicians, metaphysicians, and other men of learning.
If God is infinite, then within his Being all things he must enfold,
Which may explain some of mankind's deepest yearnings.

The craving to be at one with himself and the world at large
Could be because dependent beings have a common
        sustaining source.
The continuous, relentless search to find out who or
        what is in charge—
Because he's drawn to an all-pervading force.

Often, man looks within his consciousness, not certain of what
        there he'll find;
Probing for pointers, causes, clues, and starters, however small.
A psychological pot holder, penetrating deep recesses of his mind.
A finite response to an infinite call?

Often, man seeks true love—the union with others in
        body and/or in mind.
A journey involving mergers in a physical or platonic form.
Yet these complex relationships reveal that love is blind.
From such fusions, children and memories are born.

Often, instinctive drives compel man to explore the cold
      nonhuman universe,
And his radio telescopes unearth strange and mysterious events.
Is all this chance chaos, or is the discovered order
      something far worse—
An explanation his intellect invents?

Was man God-created or randomly evolved from
      some primeval slime?
Is man on earth to fulfill some proper purpose,
Or just a paleontologist's enigma, lost in eons of time,
A clumsy clown in a cruel, cognitive circus?

In Being in Being, philosophers of East and West can unite,
And introspection and altruism can almost mean the same.
The ideas of loving God and self in others appears to
      be quite right,
For it gives life meaning—an ultimate aim.

Someone once asked if "Disinterested Love?" was a palinode,
that is, a poem in which the writer retracts a view or sentiment
expressed in a former poem. In this case, "Motivation," p. 21.

"Disinterested Love?" does not retract but rather questions
some of the assertions made in "Motivation." To that extent, it
is not a palinode.

July 1987

Disinterested Love?

(A variation of "Motivation")

How often have you felt the need
To give yourself in thought, word, and deed
To someone, to something, an ideal?

Are these feelings the seeds of love
Planted in man's nature from above—
Flowering in peace and leading to good?

Are they indeed in essence pure,
Existing, thus, to provide the cure,
To the present mass disease of hiding behind a selfish door?

Or are they merely pangs of greed,
Urges of an egocentric breed—
Food on which the inner self may feed?

Or do they show man's weaker side,
A wilting whimp with no sense of pride,
Whose innermost strength has decayed and died?

Should man expect a nil return
And reject what gains his deeds may earn?
Is this what Christ wished all men to learn?

Just give to those who are in need.
The message is there for all to heed!
And to true self-knowledge will it lead?

Love is the coming together of two people whilst, at the same time, each maintains autonomy.

The two complement each other in a wholesome relationship.

While we fuse, we need to be ourselves. Therein lies the paradox!

August 1987

A Lover's Paradoxical Plea

Let us lose ourselves once more in love tonight,
Exude our beings in spasms of sheer delight.
Let us each become part of a greater whole,
Through the furious fusion of body and soul.

Let us find ourselves once more in love tonight.
Lift the blinds that mar the moments of clear insight.
Let us become more open and thus enable
Truth to replace what is false, fact what is fable.

Larissa was fourteen and beginning to search for her own identity. She needed space and secure support in her struggle to become more independent.

As a child, I recall spinning tops that had a central handle which, when pumped, sent the top off on its gyrations. When the handle was touched, the top lost its equilibrium and balance and quickly toppled. The skill in moving the top lay in gentle touches on the side.

December 1988

JIM MEEHAN

Teenagers Are Tops

Teenagers are like tops spinning.
Too much parental interference can lead to a fall.
What they need is balanced steering
To help them keep their eye on the ball.

The people we love are never far away.

Like cream on the top of milk, their images rise from the depths of our psyche to the level of consciousness to be enjoyed.

March 1990

Obsessed

When steeped in my work or out walking
I often call you to mind
And take pleasure in guessing
Just how you're spending your time.

When lost in a world of ideas
With my head high in the clouds,
Your face suddenly appears,
Your voice not terribly loud.

When wrapped in the warmth of your body
With your will welded to mine,
Lovers meant always to be
For all, yes, all of our time.

After forlorn attempts to express the notion of love, I had reduced my thinking to the fact that ultimately, it is tied up with the mystery that is God.

God is three persons in relationship. God is love. God is a loving relationship. One nature with three independent persons mysteriously interdepending.

Christmas 1990

Wherein Lies Love

Wherein lies love, my friends—
    wherein, wherein?
In the mystery of God's Three Persons—
    therein, therein, therein.

On a flight from Chicago to Lincoln, I was thinking about some ideas proposed by Dr. William E. Hall and Dr. William Glasser on basic human needs and drives. Both stress the internal need to be significant, which is achieved by recognition from others in good relationships. We are nobody until somebody recognizes our worth.

This is another poem I wrote at Easter time.

Easter 1992

Reality

We all need to feel significant.
It's part of the human predicament.
To give and receive recognition
Is right at the heart of man's mission.

We all need to feel some worth.
That was the point of our birth.
We should have entered the earth
Through love. To be valued, not hurt.

Let's become one of life's participants—
Achieve things and not be indifferent.
Improve the human condition.
Give something back in addition.

We all need to be resurrected,
And when given new life to direct it,
To listen to Christ's invectives,
And care for the underprotected.

Perhaps we need to accept our complexity and mixed emotions and contradictions and not get too concerned about inner tensions.

We need not expect people to be simple and easily slotted into pigeon holes.

May 1992

There's More…

There's more to you than meets the eye,
There's more than tears when you cry.
There's more to you than what you show,
There's more to you than others know.

There's more to words than what is said,
There's more to following than being led.
There's more to kissing than touching lips,
There's more to satire than pointed quips.

There's more to alms than in the giving,
There's more to life than just in living.
There's more to know than what appears,
There's more to emotions that elude ideas.

So, to your thoughts and feelings be ever true,
That in your actions you are really being you.

Something special happened one morning. The verses record it all, or rather all that I could express.

June 1992

A Poetic Release

There's something inside me that wants to get out,
A lot of love under pressure—steam wanting a spout.
It's whirling inside and it's looking for words,
It's got something to say and it wants to be heard.

So I listen in silence—there's no one about,
First a faint whisper that turns to a shout.
And after a while and after much mumbling,
On to the page the words come tumbling.

I feel very happy and I'm beginning to cry,
It's a beautiful feeling—I can't explain why.
Emotions stirring and a feeling of peace,
I can only express it as a poetic release.

It's gone now and I wonder whether I'll ever convey,
Its intensity and beauty, what it wanted to say.
Perhaps next time when it begins to boil,
The seeds will flower through much richer soil.

Relating involves risk taking. When learning to swim, we reach a point when we need to let go of the handrail and trust the bouyancy of the water. With self-disclosure, there comes a time when we need to cast caution to the winds, abandon our inhibitions, and trust that others will accept us and our vulnerability.

June 1992

Flow

It's never too late to relate,
You're never too old to unfold.
Just open your heart,
That'll do for a start,
Let go. Don't try to control.

The difference between using people and loving people lies in the real object of our motivation.

Are we interested more in our own benefit or more in the benefit of the other person?

The former involves using others, the latter in loving others.

August 1992

Manipulation's Antidote

Love requires that we give ourselves to others,
To our fellow man, our sisters and brothers.
Love grows by giving it away,
Love dies by keeping others at bay.

Only by deeds can we come to believe,
That the more you give, the more you receive.
But if you invest in others only for a return,
No love as interest will be earned.

Deep in us all, the message must be impressed,
When in others we want truly to invest.
That only when the other person is the center of concern,
Will the flame of love within us truly burn.

After listening to a southern American pastor one Sunday morning after Mass, I was so impressed by what he said, I put his ideas into verse.

The pastor was a wise octogenarian, whose name I cannot recall.

August 1992

Forever Today

If I could live my life over, what could I do or say
That would make any difference to my life today?
The actions of the past we can never undo
Whether right or wrong, good or bad, false or true!

If we could add the fears of the future to the regrets
      of yesterday,
It would make the strongest falter and stumble in their way.
We have only the now of time to do what we have to do,
To love more and better to really pay our dues.

Now, we should listen to God's voice and what he has to say,
And not put off 'til tomorrow what can be done today.
Now, we should be kind to others and give a
      sincere thank-you,
To those who love us dearly and estranged
      relationships renew.

Now, we should aspire for God's heights, though we have
      feet of clay,
And progress to perfection, helping others
      along the way.

Now, we should forgive offenders and accept
    forgiveness too.
We'll find God everywhere; God leaves many, many clues.

We can be born again as Christians every single day
And choose with God's helping hand the role we wish
    to play.
We should be generous and not just paddle our own canoe.
There's room in heaven for each passenger and every
    member of the crew!

Some selfish person annoyed me.
I used my pen like a weapon!

December 1992

Egocentric's Epigram

Some people don't really seem to bother
Living in the world of *I-other*.
They really appear content to be
In the lonely world of *I-me*,
Only ever saying "hello" to their own ego.

The essence of bodily existence and the nature of relationships ebb and flow in common.

January 1993

I wrapped an old idea in new verse.

February 1993

The Breath of Life

Without a doubt. . .
My body will die if I only breathe in and don't breathe out.

It is indeed also true. . .
That I'll die as a person if I think only of me
    and little of you.

Sophistry

After years of erudite chatter,
Two philosophers were finally inclined,
When asked "What is mind?" to say "No matter,"
When asked "What is matter?" to say "Never mind."

These words captured how I felt on Maureen's fiftieth birthday.

March 1993

Maureen

If ever man was loved by woman—
      then surely me!
If ever woman was loved by man—
      then surely thee!
If ever two were one—
      then surely we!

Dr. Hall exemplifies how to use time effectively. I put his words and ideas into this verse.

April 1993

Time, the Only Leveler

You can spend your time wisely or waste it like a fool.
You can never get it back when gone—that's
     nature's golden rule.
There are fourteen hundred and forty minutes given
     to everyone every single day,
To sleep, to think, to feel, and much to do and say.
Please, whatever you decide, don't fritter yours away!

Mutual trust lies at the heart of good relationships and is, in turn, based on a deep knowledge and understanding of others, unlike gullibility, which is based on a superficial or surface knowledge.

May 1993

Trust or Bust

What so often makes a relationship go bust?
What, if not found, means a relationship is lost?
What is not desirable but also a must?
The cementing ingredient is mutual trust.

Again, a call to accept differences within ourselves—the paradoxes, contradictions, mixed emotions, and outcomes.

July 1993

Opposites

When very happy we often cry,
To grow, to self we must die.
While a lot of me appears to be the same
All around is the permanence of change.
Value from suffering often emanates
Like the perfume of crushed roses
     or wine from crushed grapes.
Before the Resurrection—the cross,
Before being found, being lost.

Yet another verse that enshrines the teaching of Dr. Hall.

August 1993

It is not possible to love too much. To love is to become
God-like and is, in itself, positive and transforming.

September 1993

Good Relationships

Relationships begin by your response to the
    existence of another.
Do you really care or don't you bother?
They are much wider than self in scope.
Any good relationship always benefits you both.

Love's Efficacy

How long does it take true love to work—
    at first sight or never?

Perhaps so for the loved one, but for the lover—
    instantly, always, and ever.

On retreat at Mount Saint Bernard Abbey, one of the
Cistercian monks, who wishes to remain anonymous,
introduced me to the work of a Jesuit priest, Father John
Powell, who impressed me greatly, especially when speaking of
love in action. I wrote this verse as a result.

October 1993

God Really Is Love

God is love, that's what he does.
That's what gives my God a buzz.

God loves me for who I am,
Not for what I do or can.

God is love, and that love shows
Neither limits—nor provisos.

God is love, that's all God does.
That's why God became one of us.

You can meet with my God too
In loving self and others as God loves you.

As I reflected on the mind-body problem, I reviewed René Descartes' dictum, "I think, therefore, I am."

Regarding this to be true in part only, I extended and varied the theme.

November 1993

Descartes Extended

I scheme and I plan.
I search and I scan.
I think, therefore, I am.

I laugh when I can.
I cry, though a man.
I feel, therefore, I am.

I work with my hands.
My word is my bond.
I act, therefore, I am.

I think, feel, and act.
Therefore, I am.

Another Jesuit priest, Father Gerard Hughes, impressed me by his writing. While reading his book, *God of Surprises*, the title for this book occurred to me and the following verse ensued.

November 1993

Hearts Have Reasons

Hearts have reasons not so easy to find.
Body and spirit being so inextricably entwined.
This is not an area of clear black and white.
Deep in the psyche, feelings, emotions, and thoughts
      merge and unite.
Gut reactions could be nut reactions in disguise.
Intuition polysyllogisms cut down to size.
Impulse the brain's parallel processing gone wild,
Creative spontaneity is reason's real child.
Hearts have reasons that we can't always find.
As an engine is to power, so is the body to the mind?

Once again, some ideas of Dr. Hall underlie the structure of this poem.

When writing this commentary, I realized that I had not included God. However, this is not entirely true, because it is in loving ourselves and other people unconditionally that we come in contact with and experience true love, true God.

I recognize that people can also experience and relate to God in other ways, so to that extent, there is an omission.

December 1993

Invest With Interest

Between people, things, and ideas,
     we all have to choose.
What we value will win our time,
     others in proportion will lose.

Is our treasure in what we can touch,
     smell, hear, see, and feel,
Amassing possessions and objects,
     even people, who appeal?

Or are we lost in a world of ideas and thoughts,
Discerning "existences" and "essences," "musts" and "oughts"?

Just as love over faith and hope is the greatest
     of spiritual gifts,
Should people over things and ideas be mankind's
     center of interest?

People are things who can add to their own value
     with the passing of years
By adding to the value of others with deeds
     and the sharing of things and ideas.

Father Powell's analogy of the sun to represent God's love
inspired me to write these verses.

December 1993

The Sun God

It comes as no surprise to me
To see why primitive man
Identified his deity
In the shining sun.

Its light enables us to see
Whatever its rays fall on.
Faith reveals the Trinity;
God is Three in One.

The sun's release of energy
Goes on and on and on.
God loves eternally;
It's all God's ever done.

The sun beams down incessantly
On those who choose to bathe.
God's unconditional charity
Wants us to want to be saved.

During Lent of 1994, yet another Jesuit priest, Father Alban Byron, came to our parish to give a series of talks on "The Gift of Marriage" by way of celebration, enrichment, and encouragement.

You will notice his influence in several subsequent poems.

February 1994

Love Is Not…

Love is not just an emotion or a feeling
Given only to those we find appealing.

Love is not manipulation or using
A game of one winning and another losing.

Love is not selfish or grabbing,
A matter of consuming or having.

Love is a process of relating,
The mysterious interdependence of
    I-other celebrating.

The American Indians used to regard it as very important for an Indian to walk in the moccasins of other Indians.

Empathy is not a matter of saying, "If I were you" or "In your shoes, I would do so and so."

Rather, empathy involves appreciating how the other person would behave, feel, and think.

April 1994

Empathetic Steps

When stepping on each other's toes, our shoes
    need not lose their shine.

When walking in another's shoes, I must
    first get out of mine!

In December 1990, I wrote a verse that was brought up to date. The original verse was written like this:

If we could listen actively to our every word and sigh,
Would I see you as you do and you me as I?

If we could watch each other carefully when we laugh and cry,
Would I feel as you feel and you sense as I?

No matter what the answers, we can do no more than try!

April 1994

Empathy

If we could listen actively to our every word and sigh
Would I see you as you do and you me as I?

If we could watch each other carefully when
    we laugh and cry,
Would I feel as you feel and you sense as I?

If we could walk in each other's shoes
    and not be passers-by,
Would I see the world as you do and you
    the world as I?

Active listening and self-disclosure will
    lead by and by
To a deeper understanding—seeing more
    than eye to eye.

A radio program on blood donors, blood transfusion, and blood groups prompted me to write "Love Donors."

April 1994

Love Donors

God is love—God wills our greatest good.
Love is in our blood.

Love donors we are called to be,
Transfusing charity.

Love self first—then love's group discover
That of being "positive other."

When a party, not a funeral, takes part inside,
Then joy to others we can provide.

If our pot is full and brimming over,
Love cascades to another.

Love donors will our greatest good.
Love is in their blood.

Infinite Being—Infinite Love.

April 1994

Unending Love

Real love stories never have endings.
True love never fades away.
Three Persons on each other depending
Make sure it stays that way.

Love perceives the needs of others,
Which it then satisfies.
Real love stories are all around us.
True love will never die.

Father Powell wrote about giving in this way. I applied this approach to loving and cloaked it in rhyme.

April 1994

Through Love

Beyond loving, there is no greater thing we can do.
When we're through loving, then we're through!

The most learned people I have met are the most humble and modest. They keep their knowledge in perspective.

May 1994

More or Less

More knowledge more of the universe shows,
The greater the circle of ignorance grows.

The more we know, the more we know we don't know.
True humility is achieved by those who know this is so,
Not by those who see themselves as lower than low!

A bulb in the darkness glows.
More is lit, yet more shadows!

Infinite light, pitch-blackness goes.
Infinite knowledge, infinite love.

While it is impossible even for identical twins to empathize one hundred percent, some people get pretty close.

May 1994

Heartfelt Empathy

Your pain and joy in my heart.
Is this possible in whole or part?

Can I feel what you're going through?
How closely can I empathize with you?

I'll listen actively to what you say,
Nonjudgmentally, accepting all you convey.

You'll have my total positive regard,
Unconditionally given—not a reward.

I'll do whatever is, at the time, required.
Your greater good is all that is desired.

Your sorrows I yearn to take away,
Or you befriend, and in your sun with you make hay.

The more of you I understand,
The better fashioned my helping hand.

A memory, initially traced on my mind during my stay at Mount Saint Bernard Abbey, suddenly surfaced. It daily becomes more and more obvious to me.

May 1994

Learning to Love

Saint Bernard wrote that we are on this earth for
    one thing only,
And that is to learn to love.
This message should pervade each homily,
And in life, when push comes to shove.

In the opening verse, I echo the words put into Saint Thomas More's mouth in the judgment scene of Robert Bolt's play "A Man for All Seasons."

Knowledge and love, like a candle flame, when given to or shared with others, are not diminished in the giver. We need to take every opportunity to give them away.

September 1994

A Citizen of Utopia?

Someone who thinks none harm,
    wills none harm,
    says none harm,
    does none harm.

Someone who, in themselves, feels warm,
    is warm,
    to their neighbor warm,
    to their enemy warm.

Someone whose light shines bright and takes
    delight in the sharing of their flame,
Someone who makes a difference,
    a candle lighting other candles,
Yet whose brilliance remains the same.

Such people, though few in number, are not mere
    citizens of imagination.
They mingle among us and, preoccupied, their deeds
    and influence escape our due consideration.

Good turns often help despairing people to turn about.
The world is full of deserving causes.

September 1994

About Face

Some people's lives make them so bitter and twisted,
That often they wish they had never existed.

It's up to the rest of us to help them
        straighten themselves out,
And see them wear a smile as they face about.

I should have been baptized Thomas not James!

October 1994

Pray Hear

Are you really there?
Am I talking to fresh air,
When addressing you in prayer?

Is anybody home?
Am I talking to myself when alone,
Or leaving messages on your answer phone?

What can I hear?
There's nothing but tinnitus in my ears!
You've been reduced from three persons to an idea.

Oh, I see!
You've been trying to get through to me.
That's a door to which you don't have the key!

How do you relate?
Will I just have to wait,
Till there is not so much on my plate?

Meet you in person?
That would be awesome.
Oh, in helping. . . . What was that? . . . m'm someone!

Is there a connection between perception and faith? Often I fail to see patterns in ambiguous data. After a while, which can in cases be many years, I look again and, lo and behold, without any effort I see the pattern!

The history of the Old Testament, Christ's life, and those of his saints can be seen as mere actions. Miracles can be explained away, texts can be demythologized so we are left with the scanty remains. Yet with the eyes of faith we recognize patterns and see God in history and God in the present. Is faith driven from the bottom up or from the top down? Like perception, is it probably a bit of both?

October 1994

▶ *Leeper's Ambiguous Lady*

▼ *The Rubin Vase, Rubin 1915*

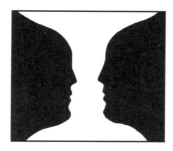

Doing What Comes Supernaturally

Suddenly, something in my brain goes click.
A pattern is perceived as if by magic.
The Rubin Vase reveals two faces.
Leeper's Lady is haggish or gracious.

Why do things look as they do?
Do I see objects and colors the same as you?
What is figure? What is ground?
How are the parts and whole together bound?

Sometimes, we notice hidden features by chance,
A sudden movement, a different glance.
Sometimes, others advise where and how to view,
Leaving the resolution up to me and you.

Many philosophers who have studied Greek and Latin
Fail to see in life's events any pattern.
People and their history are available to all,
To some providing openings, to others merely a wall.

What in the end causes us to believe?
What makes us adopt the lives we lead?
Faith reveals divine designs in reality,
And results from doing what comes supernaturally.

In human relationships, the whole is often greater than the sum of its parts. The combined effects of parties in the relationship exceed the total number of members' individual contributions. Groups, such as families or teams, can experience a life of their own, especially when striving to achieve a common goal.

While working in Cancun, Mexico, I attested such synergy in the employees of a client hotel company. It was at a time when I was exploring the latest developments concerning the genetics of personality.

The two areas of interest interacted symbiotically in my mind and emotions, and eventually I reconciled them in verse.

February 1995

Synergy

People are much closer to each other than at first it seems.
Human chromosomes hold steadfast the architecture
    of our genes.
Each single person has six billion base pairs of DNA.
Complete strangers by six million sets are kept at bay.
Sisters from brothers are merely two million pairs astray.

These biological facts do not tell the total story.
Our passion and reason add to this genetic inventory.
Genes plus empathy enable us to take a deeper view.
You are drawn close to me and I, in turn, to you.
Synergy results, and one and one become more than two.

While staying in Loveland, Colorado, which, at the time, still had Valentine's Day hearts on lamp posts, and while admiring the Twin Peaks of Mount Meeker and Longs Peak in the Rocky Mountain National Park, my mind wandered to the twin "peaks" of heart and reason.

Unlike the two mountains, which are clearly distinct and separate entities in the real world, the distinction between reason and emotion is a mental one, not a real one. The two always go together and can only be separated for the purpose of intellectual analysis. Whenever we have emotions, there are reasons for their arousal. How we cope with their expression or control in social intercourse depends on how we understand the particular circumstances that prevail. Reason is key to both the arousal stage and the coping stage of an emotion.

Society has traditionally managed to separate emotion and reason, the heart from the head. Indeed, many people regard emotions as irrational or think of them as having nothing to do with the way we think.

On the contrary, hearts have reasons. Unlike Pascal, who stated "that the reason knows nothing of," I believe that reason does know emotion. In fact, reason brought these very emotions into being and controls their disclosure, as "Passion's Parent" attempts to show.

March 1995

Passion's Parent

Meaning gives birth to emotion;
      passion is reason's real child.

The mind is a tight or free-reining parent,
      controlling or letting its child run wild.

Attainment or frustration of goals plays
      its part in what we feel.
Understanding our social environment influences
      what we control or reveal.

ABOUT THE AUTHOR

Jim Meehan was born in Liverpool, England. He is an Associate Fellow of the British Psychological Society, a psychologist whose main interest lies in exploring the positive power that human relationships have in bringing out the best in people. His work has taken him around the globe.

Whenever he gets the opportunity, he likes to walk in the mountains. Religion and philosophy are of crucial interest to him, and he enjoys conveying his thoughts and feelings in verse.

Jim's wife Maureen is a retired teacher, and his daughter Larissa is a beauty therapist. Jim currently lives and works in Lincoln, Nebraska.